Bryony

KURSK

OBERON BOOKS
LONDON

First published in 2009 by Oberon Books Ltd
521 Caledonian Road, London N7 9RH
Tel: 020 7607 3637/Fax: 020 7607 3629
e-mail: info@oberonbooks.com
www.oberonbooks.com

A catalogue record for this book is available from the British Library.

ISBN: 978-1-84002-936-9

Cover photograph by Robert Day

Printed in Great Britain by CPI Antony Rowe, Chippenham.

Characters

THE BOSS   Commanding Officer
DONNIE BLACK   Coxn/Syscon
DONNIE MAC   Radio Operator/ Officer of the
        Watch/Sonar
NEWDADMIKE   Planesman
CASANOVAKEN   Lookout/Navigator/Ops

Unseen but present characters
*… The boat is also populated by every necessary
role…so they all become, in dim light, appropriately
other necessary posts…including…*

DJ SONAR   a voice-only character in a
        locked room
CHEDDAR/DOUGIE
CHALKY/ NOBBY   talked to, teased, but
        never seen…

SOME NOTES…

Sub-running continues under everything. There is always
something else going on hence as few scenes as possible with
every actor in them, the trick is to always have one or two
people visible running the boat during the off-duty moments.

There is no gap between scenes.

/indicates dialogue intersecting.

Kursk was first performed at the Young Vic on the 3rd of June 2009 in a co-production between the Young Vic and Fuel. The cast was as follows:

THE BOSS,   Laurence Mitchell

DONNIE MAC,   Gareth Farr

DONNIE BLACK,   Ian Ashpitel

NEWDADMIKE,   Tom Espiner

CASANOVAKEN,   Bryan Dick

UNSEEN CHARACTERS,   Amanda Lawrence, Victoria Moseley, Hannah Ringham, Maria Kozlovskaya and the company of the Maly theatre.

Directors Mark Espiner and Dan Jones
Design Jon Bausor
Lighting Design Hansjörg Schmidt
Sound Design Dan Jones
Submarine Technical Adviser Bob Nunn

With Thanks to:
Surg Cdr John G Sharpley and Surg Lt Cdr James Harrison, Lt Cdr Peter Stanton-Brown, Major Mark Perrin, Cdr Jeff Tall, the Royal Navy, the MOD, the crews of HMS Torbay and HMS Trenchant, Ian Tyson, Wounded Buffalo, Martin Welton, Matt Delbridge, Shonagh Manson, Richard Oyarzabal, The Darkroom, the Arvon Foundation, The Russo-British Chamber of Commerce, the International Submariners Association, Toby Sedgwick, and all of those who have contributed to the artistic development of the piece: Mark Anstee, Simon Macer-Wright, Will Ash, Jamie Ballard, Tom Brooke, Kobna Holdbrook-Smith, Rob Cameron, Sean Campion, Alex Dunbar, Hannah Ringham, Tim Crouch, Hayley Carmichael, Brendan O'Hea and Paul Warwick.

Commissioned by the Junction Cambridge

Funded by a Wellcome Trust Arts Award **wellcome**trust

ONE – ATLANTIS BEGINS…

We are in 'non-submarine'.

A man's hands are seen, fixing a handmade paper submarine to a busy mobile of bright-kiddy-colour whales and fish.

As…

DONNIE BLACK
(*Somewhere…internally processing for the first time… some reading…*)

Atlantis

'Being set on the idea
Of getting to Atlantis,
You have discovered of
Course
Only the Ship of Fools is
Making the voyage this
Year,
As gales of abnormal force
Are predicted

> *The submarine attached, the hands make the mobile spin.*

and that
You
Must therefore be ready to
Behave absurdly enough
To pass for one of The
Boys,

> *And there is a baby's cry…she doesn't like the new submarine…*

At least appear to love
Hard liquor, horseplay and
Noise…'

> *Immediately we are on a submarine deck heading out to sea, night approaching…*

TWO – LEAVING…

Crew on deck, their ears stapled to their mobiles, making their last phone calls before mission…

Two crews: one Russian, one British, say goodbye to their off-duty lives…both in England and Russia where…

In a symphony of half-conversations…

The two languages appear to be talking to each other although the British has the foreground…the Russian ghosts…

THE BOSS, our Commanding Officer, is on the boat during this… slowly walking and checking everything…a finger wiped along here…a plug plugged in there…more ritual than actual…

As…

NEWDADMIKE
(*To mobile…his wife…*) How is she?
Is she awake?
What's she doing?
Is she?
That's her first smile!
her first smile!
Her first smile!
Groundbreaking!

    A RUSSIAN FATHER far away on another seaboard…ghosts this…

RUSSIAN FATHER
Hello…?
Who's *this????*
Sergei?
Sergei!!!
Is that my *clever* son?
Is that my clever son answering the phone?
Yes!
I see you *can* answer the telephone now!
Clever Boy!
Very Clever Boy
Now…Clever Boy…

I want you to do something for Papa…
Get Mama
Get Mama, Sergei.
I want to speak to Mama
Get Mama, Sergei…
Please…good boy…get Mama…
I want to say goodbye to Mama
And then I'll say goodbye to you, Sergei…
Sergei
Go get Mama
I want to say goodbye to Mama

NEWDADMIKE
Oh *no* her first smile!!!!
I should be there!!!
I should be…
Love…? Michelle…?
Put her ear near the phone…
No put her ear near the phone
I want her to remember my…

DONNIE MAC
(*To his wife…*) Are you looking at the switches?

Under.   The.   Stairs.

Are you looking at them?

Right…see the switch on the *far* left?

Off mobile…

Jesus *Wept!*

> *On another seaboard…a RUSSIAN WIFE…ghosts…*

RUSSIAN WIFE
…which switch?

*Yes…*I am looking at all the switches now!

Yes. The one on the far left.

Yes… I am trying it *now.*

Nothing.

Nothing at all.

Well…you said…alright…
I'm trying the next one…wait…*wait* I'm trying this one!!!

No. That doesn't do anything either.

Okay
I am going to try every one in turn…

Don't shout at me
Don't *shout*
I am trying my hardest!

Why don't you *fix* these things before you leave????

NEWDADMIKE
(*To his newborn daughter…*) Hello…
Hello sweetness its Daddy
Daddy's talking to you yes he is yes he is…now…
Daddy's going away for a bit
And he's going to miss you he's going to miss your ootiful
bootiful little-wittle face and your little plumptious body

DONNIE MAC
Okay…try that one
The one on the far left…

Try it now

    Off…

Jesus Wept Tears of *Blood!*

NEWDADMIKE
…It's only twelve weeks

DONNIE MAC
(*On…*) What do you mean… 'Nothing'???

What do you mean 'Nothing at all'???

Well you said it was the…okay okay okay
Forget the switch on the far left…

Try the switch *next* to the far left switch…
Well…the switch immediately *right* of the far left switch…

That doesn't do anything either?

Okay.

You need to try every one in turn…

Don't shout at me
Don't *shout*
I am doing my best…
I *am!*

I *do* try to fix these things before I leave!!!

I do!!!

NEWDADMIKE
Daddy'll see you in twelve weeks

CASANOVA KEN
(*Mobile…*) It's me.
Your *Big* Boy
Are you missing me??
What are you doing?
Oh, I'm picturing it…that's cruel that's very cruel
Are you?
All by yourself?
I wish I could be there doing that to you…
Do you?
Tell me how much.

    Off mobile…

This is cruelty to dumb animals!

    In Russia meanwhile…ghosts…

RUSSIAN LOVER
It's me.
How are you?
What are you doing?
Are you?
I wish I could be there doing that *to* you…

Do you?
Tell me how much.

What are you wearing?
Go slower

Describe it

Yes…

You're wearing the *black* one…?

Tell me how it feels against your skin

Yes

Yes

I wish I were with you there too.

DONNIE BLACK
(*On mobile…*) What I want to know is this…
Has the twelve weeks got to be …
Can I take longer to complete this module if I have issues
About delivering any assignments…?

I'm in the armed forces…

CASANOVAKEN
(*On mobile…*) ok

What *uniform* are you wearing for this procedure?

O sweet Jesus

Go slower
Describe it

Yes…
You're wearing ?
…the one…?

    Off mobile.

Oh dear sweet Jesus…

DONNIE BLACK
(*On mobile…*) I can't tell you

I can only say I'll be away for...some time
I can't tell you that
Or that
I can't even tell you that...sorry
There may be issues with e-mailing...
Snailmail too...

I can't say why...
Official secrets act...yes.

A RUSSIAN MOTHER ghosts...

RUSSIAN MOTHER
Did you get the biscuits?

You *did* get the biscuits!

Did you get the underwear?

Did you take the underwear with you because it's to wear
when you're...
You *didn't* take the...
But it was to wear when you're...
Well...they should *let* you take different underwear...
If someone's taken the trouble to...

Never mind never mind it doesn't matter.

Did you at least take the *photographs?*

Aren't they?

Aren't they lovely?

Doesn't your father look so much better?

I can't believe they won't let you take different underwear!

CASANOVAKEN
(*On...*) Tell me how it feels against your gorgeous tits

Yes

Yes
I wish I were with you there too.

DONNIE BLACK
And also receiving feedback from my tutor…
And contacting my tutor yes
I can't say…just on a *mission* okay…?
Also delivering
My tutor-marked assignments on time…
How do I do that…?

NEWDADMIKE
Bye bye Daddy's favorite girl… Bye bye bye

DONNIE MAC
Well…*switch* off then!

CASANOVA KEN
Write to me.
Something *dirty*.

DONNIE BLACK
What course am I on…?

BA Hons Literature
SCQF level 7
Basic tools of (*He lowers his voice…*) *poetry-writing*

CASANOVAKEN
I will.

Something *filthy*.

> *A hooter sounds which makes them all shut down their mobiles at exactly the same time.*

PIPE BROADCAST
All crew to position for diving stations
All crew to position for diving stations
All crew to position for diving stations

> *Which sends them straight to their diving stations…as…*

THREE – A DANGEROUS MAN

THE COMMANDING OFFICER, THE BOSS, in his cabin, going through his rituals before taking the control room.

Chess board squared.

Books aligned.

A reminder litany to himself…

THE BOSS
This is a Trafalgar-Class Hunter Killer Submarine.

We are A Secret Weapon. Secret.

You are The Boss
You are The Captain
If something goes wrong – it will go wrong quickly
And everyone will turn to you

Breathe…

If you let uncertainty show…
It goes right round the boat.
If you don't know what to do…
Damn well pretend you do, Sunshine.

You need more than skill you need

Instinct.

And An artist's touch.

He aligns something.

What else…?

Mono*maniacal* confidence.

Puts it in his face and head.

Puts it, minimally, in his stance.

You're taking life and death decisions for 130 men and you're
on your own.
You're centre stage.
You have to give a command performance the whole trip.

No pressure then.

He's ready.

Here we are.
Here we go.

And he goes to his position as…

Everyone else is waiting for him…

Far far away, someone is ticking off names of men on a submarine…

RUSSIAN
(*In Russian…*) First compartment
Senior Midshipman Abdulkhadur Ildarov
Midshipman Alexei Zubov
Seaman Ivan Nefedkov
Seaman Maxim Borzhov
Seaman Alexei Shulgin
Senior Lieutenant Arnold Borisov
Mamed Gadjiiev

Second Compartment
Visiting from the 7th Submarine Division Headquarters:
Captain First rank Vladimir Bagriantsev
Captain Second Rank Yury Shepetnov
Captain Second Rank Viktor Belogun
Captain Second Rank Vasily Isaenkov
Captain Third Rank Marat Baygari

Crew:
Captain First Rank Gennady Lyachin
Captain Second Rank Sergei Dudko
Captain Second Rank Alexander Shubin

Everyone is in position for DIVING STATIONS…

Everyone is now impersonal, calm, in appropriate status for…

FOUR – WE DIVE… A 60 PER CENT ALTERATION TO THE WORLD

Diving stations…
The scene requires the following personnel:
The COXON – DONNIE BLACK on Ship control
The PLANESMAN – NEWDADMIKE on the Helm
NAVIGATOR – CASANOVA KEN
CO – THE BOSS
RADIO OPS – DONNIE MAC
OPS (Operations.) – Taken by CASANOVA KEN where possible
In addition:
SYS CON – DONNIE BLACK
OFFICER OF THE WATCH – DONNIE MAC
SONAR – DONNIE MAC

THE BOSS in the control room…

THE BOSS
Coxn. Take the Submarine to Diving Stations.

COXN/DONNIE BLACK
(*Repeats.*) Take the Submarine to diving Stations, aye aye Sir.

(*Picks up the microphone.*) Manoeuvring Room, Ship Control.

MANOEUVRING ROOM/VOICE OVER
Manoeuvring Room.

COXN/DONNIE BLACK
Permission for full Main Broadcast?

MANOEUVRING ROOM/VOICE OVER
Yes Please!

COXN/DONNIE BLACK
(*Makes a switch on his console, on front of George – a piece of bulky kit that helps run the submarine which the crew have affectionately given a name.*)

Diving Stations

He presses the general alarm three times.

Diving Stations, Diving Stations. DCHQ close up. All reports to DCHQ.

There are a series of reports made to DCHQ regarding all areas of the submarine and that personnel are closed up. During this period several people are moving around and taking up positions in the Control Room.

COXN/DONNIE BLACK
DCHQ. Ship Control

DCHQ/VOICE OVER
DCHQ!

COXN/DONNIE BLACK
Control Room Closed up at Diving Stations

DCHQ/VOICE OVER
Roger Control Room Closed up at Diving Stations. Captain, Sir – DCHQ.

THE BOSS
Captain!

DCHQ/VOICE OVER
The Submarine is closed up at Diving Stations!

THE BOSS
Captain Roger. Officer of the Watch. Captain.

OFFICER OF THE WATCH (OOW)/DONNIE MAC
Officer of the watch, sir

THE BOSS
Clear the Bridge, Come Below, Shut the Upper Lid!

OOW/DONNIE MAC
Clear the Bridge, Come Below, Shut the Upper Lid, Aye Aye Sir!

The LOOKOUT will appear at the bottom of the Conning Tower with various items of equipment in which is included Binoculars, Aldis Lamp, Extended lead Microphones. He will deposit them on the Chart Table area, or in a cupboard underneath it.

COXN/DONNIE BLACK
(*As he sees LOOKOUT arrive in the Control Room…*) Lookout Below

> *The LOOKOUT will now stand at the bottom of the Conning Tower and wait for the OOW to appear at the top of the tower. He will then relay what the OOW says from the tower.*

OOW/DONNIE MAC
Officer of the watch in the tower

LOOKOUT/CASANOVA KEN
(*Repeats into the Control Room…*) Officer of the watch in the tower.

OOW/DONNIE MAC
Upper Lid Shut

LOOKOUT/CASANOVA KEN
(*To the Control Room.*) Upper lid shut

OOW/DONNIE MAC
One Clip

LOOKOUT/CASANOVA KEN
(*To the Control Room.*) One clip

OOW/DONNIE MAC
One Pin

LOOKOUT/CASANOVA KEN
(*To the Control Room.*) One pin

OOW/DONNIE MAC
Two Clips

LOOKOUT/CASANOVA KEN
(*To the Control Room.*) Two clips

OOW/DONNIE MAC
Two Pins

LOOKOUT/CASANOVA KEN
(*To the Control Room.*) Two pins

> *The OOW will then appear at the bottom of the Conning Tower and proceeds to where the CO is.*

OOW/DONNIE MAC
Officer of the watch below, Upper Lid Shut, Two Clips, Two Pins

When the COXN sees the OOW in the Control Room he says:

COXN/DONNIE BLACK
Officer of the watch below. (*To the PLANESMAN.*) Shut the voice pipe

THE BOSS
Roger I have the Submarine. Is your Trim on Coxon?

DONNIE BLACK
Yes Sir.

THE BOSS
We will see! (*To NAVIGATOR on Chart Table.*) Depth below the Keel?

NAVIGATOR/CASANOVA KEN
150 meters, Sir.

THE BOSS
Very Good.

He then completes a 360 look on the Search Periscope to check any contacts.

THE BOSS
Sonar. Any contacts?

SONAR/DONNIE MAC
There are three contacts held on sonar.

Contact zero three one bearing 110, faint cavitation, slight in/out and a whine. Possible classification Warship. Bearing drawing slow right.

Second contact zero zero six bearing 180, very faint tonal contact on narrow band. No other information, bearing drawing slow left.

Third contact, zero two eight on a bearing of 090, two shafts, four blades, 110 rpm possible Merchant Vessel. Bearing drawing left.

As the Sonar report is being made the CO turns the periscope to the bearings that have been given to see if anything is visual.

THE BOSS
Nothing Visible on those bearings

OPS/CASANOVA KEN
Roger Sonar Controller, watch and report contact zero zero six

SONAR/DONNIE MAC
Roger watch and report zero zero six

THE BOSS
Does anybody in the control room know any reason why this submarine should not be dived?

Coxn pipe Diving Now

COXN/DONNIE BLACK
Pipe Diving Now, Aye Aye Sir.

> *COXN reaches for the microphone, makes a switch on the panel on the front of George.*

Diving Now, Diving Now.

THE BOSS
(*To Sys Con…*) Open 3 and 4 Main Vents

SYS CON/DONNIE BLACK
Open 3 and 4 Main Vents

> *He reaches forward and moves two switches.*

3 and 4 Main Vents Indicate Open

> *BOSS then swings the periscope to look at the stern and watch as the air leaves the ballast tanks. There is now a pause of around thirty seconds.*

THE BOSS
Open 1 and 2 Main Vents

> *BOSS then checks by periscope the forward end of the Submarine to see the air escaping. Once he is happy that the boat is starting to dive…*

Down all Masts!

SYS CON/DONNIE BLACK
Down all Masts.

> *The Sys Con puts all the Mast Control Switches to the down position and after a pause reports.*

All mast's indicate Down.

THE BOSS
6 (*Degrees.*) down 30 (*Metres.*) back to 20

COXN/DONNIE BLACK
6 down, 30 back to 20, aye aye Sir

PLANESMAN/NEWDADMIKE
6 Down, 30 back to 20, aye aye Sir.

> *PLANESMAN pushes forward on the stick and keeps it there for about 15-20 seconds before saying…*

PLANESMAN/NEWDADMIKE
6 Down achieved

> *He keeps calling the depth out in incremental metres.*

THE BOSS
Roger 6 Down

> *COXN leans forward and sets the depth on the digital depth gauge.*

> *As the Submarine starts to get underwater the COXN takes the microphone.*

COXN/DONNIE BLACK
All compartments report Hatches from Fwd.

> *There is then a complete listing, by report of the hatches and if they are DRY/WET/LEAKING. This could be reported via the control room to allow for dialogue to continue until the Submarine gets to depth. The only other voice would be the depth being called.*

> *Here the list of Russian submariners on board Kursk continue to be listed…*

COXN/DONNIE BLACK
Captain, Sir all hatches dry.

THE BOSS
Roger Hatches, shut the lower lid.

COXN/DONNIE BLACK
On depth 30 meters, 6 up keep 20 meters

> *THE PLANESMAN then reverses planes and reports.*

PLANESMAN/NEWDADMIKE
6 up achieved.

> *He then calls out the depth on the way back to 20 meters. At around 22 meters the CO orders.*

THE BOSS
Raise Search until I say well.

SYS CON/DONNIE BLACK
Raise Search until you say well

> *He operates the switch to raise Search, looks over his right shoulder whilst doing it.*

Search Going up

THE BOSS
Well! Depth now.

COXN/DONNIE BLACK
On Depth 20 meters

THE BOSS
Keep 22 meters

COXN/DONNIE BLACK
Keep 22 meters

THE BOSS
Shut All Main Vents

SYS CON/DONNIE BLACK
Shut all Main Vents

> *He leans forward and operates the 4 switches.*

All Main Vents Indicate Shut

THE BOSS
Roger Main Vents

Coxn, Trim Check you have the planes and Bubble

COXN/DONNIE BLACK
Roger Trim Check, Sir

Orders the PLANESMAN.

Midships the Planes and Bubble for a Trim Check

PLANESMAN/NEWDADMIKE
Midships the Planes and Bubble

He will then make sure that the Bubbles and the Planes and Rudder are amidships and report.

Planes, Rudder and Bubble Amidships

The COXN now assesses the trim of the Submarine in all directions Up, Down, Left, Right, Forward and Backward! When he is happy with the Trim...

COXN/DONNIE BLACK
Captain, Sir, Coxn

THE BOSS
Captain

COXN/DONNIE BLACK
Happy with the Trim, Sir

THE BOSS
Roger, Lower search. Carry on Planing. 10 down keep 60 meters come left steer zero six five, revolutions one six

COXN/DONNIE BLACK
Lower Search. Carry on Planeing. 10 down, keep 60 meters, come left steer 065, revolutions one six. Aye, aye Sir

To the PLANESMAN/NEWDADMIKE.

10 down keep 60 meters, Port 10 steer 065

He then rings on 16 revolutions.

PLANESMAN/NEWDADMIKE
10 down, keep 60 meters, Port 10 steer 065

He then calls out the depth and the degrees to course until he says.

On course 065 on depth 60 meters

THE BOSS
(*When he is happy that the boat is safe.*) Coxon fall out from
Diving Stations go to the Watch

COXN/DONNIE BLACK
Fall out from Diving Stations, go to the Watch, Roger Sir.

COXN picks up the microphone.

Do you hear there, Fall out from Diving Stations. First Watch,
Watch Dived, Patrol Quiet State Damage Control State 3.

*And within this somewhere…weaving in and out, all the names of
the men on Kursk…*

All men move to somewhere else in the boat where they have
a stowing task…

*Each one hits his head, bangs his arm, bops his knee on a ladder/
above/below pipe with differing degrees of hurt and irritation…*

DONNIE BLACK
(*To far end of boat…*) Nice haircut, Cheddar!
Been in prison?

Biffs into…

Ow!

DONNIE MAC
(*To aft…*) No more bloody *women* for six weeks, Dougie!

Perfect! *Exactly!*

Biffs into…

Fuck!

NEWDADMIKE
Oh bloody hell!
Alright Chalkie?

Alright Nobby?

CASANOVA
Hello again, Unbearable Space and Luxury!

Ouch!

DONNIE MAC
Always bleeding forget how bleeding cramped this cramped bleeder is!

DONNIE BLACK
Please don't break the Boss's boat…

ALL
No Coxn
Sorry Coxn…

DONNIE MAC
(*To NEWDADMIKE.*) Let's have a look at her then, 'NewDad' Lead in his pencil after all…

    NEWDADMIKE gives him the finger…

DONNIE BLACK
(*Same time…to CASANOVAKEN…*) Good shore leave, Casanova 2000?

CASANOVAKEN
(*Austen Powers.*) 'Yeah Baby!'

DONNIE BLACK
Let's have a look at her then, *international man of mystery*…

    And photographs…

DONNIE MAC
(*Fake…*) aawwwwwwwww

DONNIE BLACK
(*Fake…*) oooooooooooh

BOTH DONNIES
Name?

CASANOVAKEN
Maria.

She gave me *this*

> *A large clanky, chromy watch…*

Never taking it off

NEWDADMIKE
Madison
Madison Emily Hannah

DONNIE MAC
(*Fake…*) lovely name

NEWDADMIKE
Michelle's choice fuck off

DONNIE BLACK
Well, I expect she's beautiful *inside*

DONNIE MAC
Pity, lookswise, she's taken after you not Michelle

NEWDADMIKE/CASANOVAKEN
(*Both simultaneously give the finger and…*) How beautiful is that/
she???

> *BOSS passes close to them…*

> *ALL salute.*

ALL
Morning, Sir.
Lovely Day for it.

THE BOSS
August Bank Holiday weather.
Don't forget your sunscreen.

ALL
No sir.
Or our sunglasses, sir.
Beach towels.

THE BOSS
As long as you're fully prepared.
Everything you need for a day at the beach.

ALL
Yes sir

He goes to his cabin.

All crew have unpacked…

All holding a mixed tape…

ALL
(*Variations of…*) My mixed tape! Wait till you hear this little
baby/this bad boy
No my mixed tape!
Not kidding…mine is *stellar*!
Mine is fucking *genius!*

But CASANOVAKEN wins the race to the tape deck…

The tape plays 'Maria' by Blondie

CASANOVAKEN sings along

Then

Everybody joins

THE TWO DONNIES substituting 'Diarrhoea' for 'Maria'.

FIVE – NO PRESSURE

Meanwhile…

*THE BOSS is setting up his chess pieces into the middle of a
game as…*

THE BOSS
Okay…
We were at… (*Piece of paper with…places…*) rook bishop queen
White bishop pawn bishop pawn pawn
Pawn white bishop knight pawn…white pawn pawnwhite
knight…whites pawn pawn pawn pawn pawn…castle
queen…

(*We will all recognize the board now in play for the last sixty moves
of the Amber Tournament Carlsen/Aronian game…!*)

DONNIE MAC
Captain's Eyes Only sir.

THE BOSS
Oh good, our Holiday destination.

DONNIE MAC
Almost time for cocoa and biscuits sir

THE BOSS
Bedtime already?

DONNIE MAC
Milk warming up as we speak, sir

THE BOSS
Chocolate hobnobs?

DONNIE MAC
Till we run out sir…

 Exits…

THE BOSS
Okay…where are we going? What are we doing?

 Peruses orders.

 Gist is…

Proceed via the Marginal Ice Zone…to…
Barents Sea…
And (*Surprise surprise!*)

Pretend you're not there

Detect and monitor movement of Russian vessels
particularly…nuclear ballistic-missile submarines

Who will be pretending *they're* not there.

Plus
Detect and monitor also movement of any underwater activity
From any of our American friends
Who will also be pretending they're not there.

Considerable intelligence available…that Russians are about
to engage in their usual summer War Game…

Its going to be like Piccadilly fucking Circus
So
Be careful
Be very very careful

Plus side
It's summer ergo
Arctic Ocean will be calm
Minus side
Its summer ergo
Long daylight hours makes us easier to spot

Looks at the chess board.

Tricky.

Here's what we'll do…
Head for where the Arctic ice is melting…
Because…
Fresh water meeting sea water gives us differing salinity and
temperature
because
that will confuse Russian sonar…

Now…
Bishop to…

His hand hovers.

Decides.

SIX – RUSSIAN STOWAWAYS…

The bunks…we just see the heads and hands of the two DONNIES.

DONNIE MAC
Donnie!

DONNIE BLACK
What, Donnie?

DONNIE MAC
we're in deep deep trouble here…

DONNIE BLACK
We're submariners…we're always in deep deep trouble, Twat.

DONNIE MAC
Hot-bunking with Cheddar… Just found this…

He reveals a Russian multi-person doll.

In a Russian parallel universe, more Russian submariners are ticked off…

Russian voice reads the names:

Seventh compartment…
Captain-lieutenant dmitri kolsnikov…
Midshipman fanis ishmudatov…petty officer second class
Vladimir sadovoi…seaman roman kubikov…seaman Alexei
nekrasov…petty officer first class rishat zubaydullin.

DONNIE BLACK
Stowaway!

DONNIE MAC
Soviet Stowaway!

DONNIE BLACK
Even worse

Examines it and…

Oh my god…
Far worse than we thought…

DONNIE MAC
Not…

DONNIE BLACK
'Soviet Stowaways'…*Plural!*

Reveals the within nature of the doll…

More Russian submariners are ticked off…

DONNIE MAC
The boat is *crawling* with Soviet spies…

DONNIE BLACK
Cheddar's a *double* agent!

DONNIE MAC
Worse
Cheddar's a fucking moron…
'what do I *really* need on a cramped fucking sub where space is at a premium…*I know* some useless fucking Russian dolls!'…

> *And they stand the diminishing useless fucking Russian dolls in a row…*

Stand there. Don't move.

DONNIE BLACK
We've got you surrounded. We're trained killers.

DONNIE MAC
Names!

DONNIE BLACK
(*As dolls…*) Ivan Ivan Ivan Ivan Ivan Ivan Ivan Ivan and Igor…

> *List continues behind…*

DONNIE MAC
Dressing up as *women* isn't going to fool *us*, Ivan Ivan Ivan Ivan Ivan Ivan Ivan and Igor…

DONNIE BLACK
No way!
We haven't been at sea *that* long…

NEWDADMIKE
(*Voice of…*) Donnie Black!
Donnie Mac!
Shut the fuck *up!*

DONNIES
Sorry New Daddy
Nightnight New Daddy!

And they all curl foetally as...

DONNIE BLACK
(*Whispers...*) Night Ivan Ivan Ivan Ivan Ivan Ivan Igor

DONNIE MAC
(*Russian...*) spa-koy-nee no chi, comrade Donnie Black (*Phon: 'have a peaceful night'.*)

NEWDADMIKE
Two Donnies...
Shut. The. Fuck Up!

All through this exchange, in the control room...

CASANOVAKEN as NAVIGATOR... Just see his hands at the plot table...

BOSS enters control room...as

SONAR/VOICE OVER
Ops sonar controller

OPS/VOICE OVER
Ops

SONAR/VOICE OVER
Classification contact zero three two now bearing zero three six, two shafts three blades, two six zero revolutions, in out, otter boards audible, chains audible, classification medium sized fishing vessel.

OPS
Roger classification zero three two fishing vessel.

THE BOSS
How we doing Vasco?

NAV/CASANOVA
Fine sir
I've plotted a course
Assessed our possible speed
suggest alter course to 325, initially, and come up to six and half knots.

THE BOSS
What time will we be in area?

NAV/CASANOVA
Approximately, 30 hours sir

THE BOSS
OK, come up to 8 knots and give me an updated time in area.

NAV/CASANOVA
(*Does some mental arithmetic. BOSS waits.*) That'll have us there
about five hours earlier, sir.

THE BOSS
Roger that. Carry on.

NAV/CASANOVA
Ship control Navigator. Come left, steer 325 revolutions for 8
knots.

COXN/VOICE OVER
Come left steer revolutions for 8 knots. Roger sir.

He increases revs on George…

PLANESMAN/VOICE OVER
Port 15 steer 325 (*Turns wheel.*) 15 degrees of port wheel on.

COXN/VOICE OVER
(*To NAVIGATOR.*) Submarine at 8 knots, sir.

NAV/CASANOVA
Roger 8 knots

PLANESMAN/VOICE OVER
20 degrees to course,

10 degrees to course

on course 325

COXN/VOICE OVER
(*To NAVIGATOR.*) On course 325

THE BOSS
(*Picks up phone and speak to MANOEUVRING ROOM.*)
Manoeuvring room, captain

MANOEUVRING ROOM/VOICE OVER
Manoeuvring room, sir

THE BOSS
Permission for full main broadcast

MANOEUVRING ROOM/VOICE OVER
Yes Please

THE BOSS
This is the captain speaking.

This is what I can tell you.

We're heading on a northerly course towards the arctic ice.

Straight towards the north pole for a little fresh air.

Everybody cheers.

Those of you who still haven't got your blue nose certificates…

NEWDADMIKE/CASANOVA both cheer…

this is your chance…
We'll be ticking off various routines on arrival…
Once achieved…
We'll proceed to The Barents Sea
Where we will monitor a Russian naval exercise…

First stop then…

The North Pole.

Visit Father Christmas.

SEVEN – SECRET POETRY

DONNIE MAC and NEWDADMIKEasleep.

DONNIE BLACK covertly gets out a pamphlet…

Meanwhile, words and commands of the boat operating continue.

DONNIE BLACK
(*Reads;.*) 'Have you ever wanted to write poetry but

Felt mystified about how to go about it? This 12-week online course
Suitable for beginners
Introduces you in a gradual and accessible way to the basic 'tools of the trade' Through examples, exercises and games, you will practise poetic devices and methods, get ideas for subject matter, and learn how to edit your work. You will eventually write in a variety of forms from the haiku to the sonnet and in a range of styles including satire and parody. The course will also enhance your reading skills and increase your ability to appreciate contemporary poetry…' okay…one read

'*Atlantis* by W H Auden…. see if you can find any sort of pattern to the layout of words…'

THE BOSS
Ship control captain.

COXN/VOICE OVER
Ship control sir

THE BOSS
Keep 250 metres

COXN/VOICE OVER
Keep 250m aye aye sir

THE BOSS
Let me know when you're on depth

>   *As…*

DONNIE BLACK
(*Reads, very quickly, the first verse…he's read it before…*)

'Being set on the idea
Of getting to Atlantis,
You have discovered of
Course
Only the Ship of Fools is
Making the voyage this
Year,

As gales of abnormal force
Are predicted
and that
You
Must therefore be ready to
Behave absurdly enough
To pass for one of The
Boys,
At least appear to love
Hard liquor, horseplay and
Noise…'

Pattern???

> *Elsewhere, on watch, at a machine bank, CASANOVA takes a large bag of Werther's originals out of some secret stowed place, takes one out, puts it in his mouth…restows the bag. Eats as he examines, very fondly, his big chromy watch…then kisses it…*

> *Slower now…*

> *Meanwhile…*

> *The boat dives.*

COXN/VOICE OVER
Roger, sir. Manoeuvring, ship control.

MANOEUVRING ROOM/VOICE OVER
Manoeuvering room

COXN/VOICE OVER
Submarine going to 250m

MANOEUVRING ROOM/VOICE OVER
Roger submarine going to 250m

COXN/VOICE OVER
(*Leans forward and sets revolutions for 12 knots.*) Officer of the watch Cox'n.

OOW/VOICE OVER
Officer of the watch

COXN/VOICE OVER
Revolutions for 12 knots set

OOW/VOICE OVER
Roger

COXN/VOICE OVER
(*To PLANESMAN.*) 8 down keep 250m

PLANESMAN/VOICE OVER
8 down keep 250m

150

160

170

PLANESMAN/VOICE OVER
(*To COXN…*) On depth 250m

COXN/VOICE OVER
Officer of the watch 250m

SONAR/VOICE OVER
Ops sonar controller

OPS/VOICE OVER
Ops

SONAR/VOICE OVER
Possible narrow band contact – array unstable. Will report when array steady.

OPS/VOICE OVER
Ops roger.

SONAR/VOICE OVER
Ops sonar controller

OPS/VOICE OVER
Ops

SONAR/VOICE OVER
Faint tonals in 2 beams – continuing to analyse.

And DONNIE BLACK at the same time reads…

DONNIE BLACK
'Should storms, as may well happen
Drive you to anchor a week
In some old-harbour city
Of Ionia, then speak
With her witty scholars
Men
Who have proved there
Cannot be
Such a place as Atlantis
Learn their logic, but
Notice
How its subtlety betrays
Their enormous grief
Thus they shall teach you
The ways
To doubt that you may believe…'

DONNIE BLACK realizes they are diving…

Bit steep, boys

Aloud…

Let's pitch camp here and climb the rest in the morning

There's some sleeping goes on.

DONNIE MAC gets out of bunk, still asleep, gets back in other way.

Then.

Signal of shift change.

TWO DONNIES roll out of bunks.

NEWDADMIKE and CASANOVA roll into same bunks.

EIGHT – WATER IN THE PEOPLE TANK

DONNIE MAC puts on his mixed tape…as…

DONNIE MAC
And it's time for a Donnie Mac mixed tape!

EVERYBODY
(*Groans...*) not a Donnie Mac mixed tape!...

Tape plays 'Yellow' by Coldplay

DONNIE MAC sings along

NEWDADMIKE joins in

then

CASANOVAKEN

They all go large

NEWDADMIKE gets up, shower equipment...heads to shower.

CASANOVA gets up, wearing only his watch, holding his genitals, which are in a state of arousal, goes into THE HEADS...

NEWDADMIKE/DONNIE MAC perform a double shower singing uber-large now...

COXN/DONNIE BLACK
What's going on in here?

DONNIE MAC
Dhobi, Coxn.

COXN/DONNIE BLACK
You get in
Get wet
Switch off tap
Soap yourself
Rinse off
That's it

DONNIE MAC/NEWDADMIKE
Sir yes sir

COXN/DONNIE BLCK
Not considering a Hollywood shower in there are you lads?

NEWDAD/DONNIE MAC
No Coxn.
Three seconds toppers.

They continue singing.

DONNIE BLACK
(*Quotes...*) 'you have discovered...only the Ship of *Fools*
Is making the voyage this time of year...' ah, a *pattern...*

> *Lights on NEWDADMIKE baby photo is now taped up somewhere.
> There's a regular metallic clicking sound...*

THE BOSS
What's that sound, Coxn?

COXN/DONNIE BLACK
Singing sir.

THE BOSS
No. Clicking sound.
Stop the singing...

COXN/DONNIE BLACK
Stop the singing lads.

Tape...

> *Singing...tape stopped.*

> *They listen.*

> *It is serious.*

COXN/DONNIE BLACK
No idea, sir.

Sonar controller, ship control

SONAR/VOICE OVER
Sonar controller

COXN/DONNIE BLACK
Captain's heard unexplained noise.
Is there anything on sonar?

SONAR/VOICE OVER
Will investigate and report.

> *As they wait...*

THE BOSS
Don't like it.

COXN/DONNIE BLACK
Nor me, sir

SONAR/VOICE OVER
Have investigated noise – seems to be coming from inside the submarine.
Showing on sonar probably forward of the fin.
Sound ceased.
Checking recordings and will report back.

THE BOSS
(*On broadcast.*) Okay
All men
Listen carefully
I'm about to
Extract
and employ
the most dangerous weapon on board …

He reaches in his pocket…takes out,

Holds up his index finger.

Dirty boys
Time to see if we all understand the term
'Deep Cleaning'

Be afraid be very afraid…

Runs it along surfaces…

It's okay.

Then.

Behind…

Finds.

Dirt Coxn

COXN/DONNIE BLACK
Yes sir.

THE BOSS
Dirt

COXN/DONNIE BLACK
Yes Sir.

THE BOSS
I want to be able to eat my breakfast dinner tea off every surface of this boat.

COXN/DONNIE BLACK
Sir

THE BOSS
Every surface…

There is an unplugged plug…

THE BOSS plugs it in…

Find out which tosser left *that* uplugged

COXN/DONNIE BLACK
Sir

Until…

THE BOSS
What's that water?
What's this water????
What's the golden rule…?

ALL
Absolutely No Water In The People Tank!

THE BOSS
(*It is serious…*) If it's fresh water somebody's in for a bollocking…

He puts his finger in it…

If it's sea water…

Tastes it.

fresh

Bollocking

To two Showerers…

Get out here.

They do. Smartish. Sloshing water about.

DONNIE MAC/NEWDADMIKE
It was *him*, Sir.
Overdoing the dhobi.

THE BOSS
Not funny.
Not clever.

DONNIE MAC/NEWDADMIKE
No sir.
Sorry sir.

THE BOSS
Not funny *at* all.

Three things I don't like idiots playing fast and loose with…
Food
Bog roll
Water
Mop it up

DONNIE MAC/NEWDADMIKE
Sir

THE BOSS
And Get dressed.
You look like a gay porn video.

He moves on to…

DONNIE MAC/NEWDADMIKE clean and polish as…

NEWDADMIKE
(*Very quiet.*) When has the Boss seen a gay porn video?

DONNIE MAC
Don't ask don't tell. Darling.

Fake camp air kiss.

SONAR/VOICE OVER
Ops sonar controller

OPS/VOICE OVER
Ops

SONAR/VOICE OVER
Possible narrow band contact – array unstable. Will report when array steady.

OPS/VOICE OVER
Ops roger.

SONAR/VOICE OVER
Ops sonar controller

OPS/VOICE OVER
Ops

SONAR/VOICE OVER
Faint tonals in 2 beams – continuing to analyse.

CASANOVAKEN at his machine, to an imaginary Maria...

CASANOVAKEN
This is me, Babe

Demonstrates his machine, his sitting position...

What, Babe?
That sign?

What I control...
Wind
Sea
Swell
Cloud
Precipitation
Visibility
Surface sea state...
Boat's safe with me, Babe...

NINE – FAMILYGRAMS [ONE]

Mess room.

*DONNIE BLACK, NEWDADMIKE, CASANOVAKEN playing
uckers…*

RUSSIAN DOLLS grouped, watching.

DONNIE BLACK
(*To dolls…*) look and learn, filthy foreign boys…look and
learn…

NEWDADMIKE
(*As dolls…*) Da…Comrade Donnie…vot is zis uckers you are
teaching us?

CASANOVAKEN
You ludo-playing bastard

DONNIE BLACK
(*As Doctor Evil from Austen Powers…*) 'Let this be a reminder to
you all that this organisation will not tolerate failure…'

DONNIE MAC enters with Familygrams…

DONNIE MAC
Two weeks!
Familygrams

Hands them to DONNIE BLACK, himself and CASANOVAKEN…

To dolls.

Nothing for you Ivan Ivan Ivan Ivan Ivan Ivan and Igor…

Sorry.

They all start to read theirs…

NEWDADMIKE
Where's mine?

DONNIE MAC
You didn't get one

You didn't get one!

NEWDADMIKE
Are you sure?

DONNIE MAC
Yes I'm sure. (*To CASANOVA.*) how's 'Diarrhoea'…?

NEWDADMIKE
I should get one. (*He exits to the radio room.*)
Michelle wouldn't not send one…

DONNIE BLACK
Weird he didn't get one.

DONNIE MAC
Weird. Yes.

> *He puts a familygram in NEWDADMIKE's place.*

DONNIE BLACK
You mean bastard

> *NEWDADMIKE arrives back…*

NEWDADMIKE
Okay…*checked* the bloody incoming roster/there *is* one for me!

DONNIE MAC
It's right there you blind bastard

NEWDADMIKE
You bastard.
Not funny.

DONNIE MAC
Quite funny
You're such a gullible bastard…

CASANOVAKEN
Can we just read what we've got in *peace*????

TWO DONNIES
Oooooooooh can we hear from *Diarrhoea*????

DONNIEMAC
40 words of *wonderful*!

> *And they read…*

45

We hear female voices interweave…

MARIA

Hi Pet Lover. Missing you loads. My Puppies also missing you, but am stroking them all time to remind them of you and fun we all had playing with your lovely balls. Little Pussy also missing you. Pierced belly button. Maria.

MRS MAC

Hope all fine with you. Got Roy from next door in. Has Fixed washing machine, loose stair rods, creaking bed, uneven bathroom tiles kitchen shelves and painted Sasha's room warm yellow. Wants no money just dinner. Hurray. Love. Deb

MICHELLE

Mum and Dad here five days see Madison. Very brown from Cyprus. Brought pram we asked for. Fantastic. Madison and me missing Daddy. We both love you loads. Mum Dad send love. Big Kiss from Madison. Big Kiss from me.

MRS BLACK

Football started. Man U. won. Hurray. Chelsea lost. Hurray. Man U. unassailable lead fingers crossed. Weather shit. Cricket rained off. Your books arrived. Extra Postage due. Paid it for you. Gran in hospital again but okay.

CASANOVA

She's had her belly button pierced/
Oh Sweet Jesus!

He heads for the HEADS.

DONNIE BLACK

Nice fruity message, Casanova…?

DONNIE MAC

Warm yellow?

She knows I hate warm fucking yellow!

NEWDADMIKE

Madison's got that pram.
The Silver Cross Oberon in the snowdrop white with navy upholstery…

DONNIE MAC
Shut *up* you *girl!*

TEN – A STRANGE NOISE

Elsewhere on the boat…

That strange rhythmical clicking sound…

THE BOSS
It's started again.!!!!
Bloody noise!!!
Is it from the same place????
Ship control make a warning pipe.

COXN/DONNIE BLACK
(*On broadcast…*) Do you hear there?

There is banging in the boat it is to cease immediately!

Everybody becomes alert and ceases making any noises.

CASANOVA emerges gingerly from the heads.

Can you hear that?

Clicking sound?

All listen.

CASANOVA
Can't hear anything, sir

DONNIE MAC
It's stopped

All listen.

No sound.

SONAR
Ops sonar controller.
Noise ceased again.
Still checking on previous recordings.

MANOEUVRE ROOM/VOICE OVER
Ship control.

COXN/DONNIE BLACK
Ship control

MANOEUVRE ROOM/VOICE OVER
work was taking place on the port turbine. As agreed at daily brief.
Have stopped work.
confirm this was source of noise.

COXN/DONNIE BLACK
Ship control roger.

THE BOSS
No it wasn't.
It wasnt Aft!
Forward!
Trace the bloody noise Forward!

SONAR
Ops sonar controller
have feeling it could be safety rail above Weapons stowage compartment on 2 deck.

THE BOSS
Somebody go check weapons on 2 deck!
(*Someone goes smartish to investigate weapons compartment on 2 deck as…*)
It's not the bloody *fridge* again?

DONNIE MAC
Fridge was fixed Sir.

THE BOSS
Check her anyway…

    DONNIE moves…

She's an old girl…but she shouldn't be fucking *clinking!*

I don't like hearing noises I don't know!

Sound room to send someone out on noise rounds.

I want this sorted!

SONAR
Roger. Sonar controller, ops

OPS/KEN
Ops

SONAR
Noise husbandry routine, forward on two deck

OPS/KEN
Roger sonar

> *CASANOVAKEN goes fwd with listening device to monitor machinery and listen audibly for any obvious sounds of the noise. Uses a hand held bit of kit which he places above and below the mount of the machinery and carefully listening with ears...*

> *As...*

> *A loud bang heard.*

> *The submarine has been hit on the fin by an unknown object.*

> *They all hit their heads on something overhanging...*

ALL
Shiiiit!!!!

COXN/DONNIE BLACK
(*On broadcast...*) loud unexplained bang external to the submarine.

> *He presses general alarm once and...*

go deep go deep go deep.

> *General alarm three times.*

Emergency stations emergency stations loud unexplained bang external to the submarine DCHQ close up – carry out phase one damage checks and report to DCHQ.

> *During this he's reached forward and put the telegraphs to half ahead and wound on revs for about 15 knots.*

PLANESMAN/NEWDADMIKE
On depth 200m.

DCHQ/VOICE OVER
Captain DCHQ

THE BOSS
Captain

DCHQ/VOICE OVER
Phase one damage control checks complete no sign of any damage to the submarine internally no injuries reported by ship's company.

SONAR
Ops sonar

OPS/KEN
Ops

SONAR
no indication of vessel on sonar

biologics audible, no other contacts.

OPS/KEN
Roger

THE BOSS
Roger, revolutions for 6 knots 10 up keep safe depth [60m]

COXN/DONNIE BLACK
10 up keep safe depth, revolutions for 6 knots roger sir (*To PLANESMAN.*) 10 up keep 60m

PLANESMAN/NEWDADMIKE
Roger 10 up keep 60m.

COXN leans forward and reduces revs to speed for 6 knots.

COXN/DONNIE BLACK
What the bleeding hell????

They all wait until...

SONAR
Just an overboard container

PLANESMAN/NEWDADMIKE
Serious Damage was only averted…
By world-class rally driving from the incredibly handsome
father-of-one…

SONAR
Ops sonar, contact 041 classified whales

And sound of whales in water…

PLANESMAN/NEWDADMIKE
Bloody whales playing whale football…
One mis-heads the container with its mighty nut…dush!

THE BOSS
No scientific evidence whales play football, Mike.

COXN/DONNIE BLACK
No sir. Wales. Famous for rugby, sir.

SONAR
They're singing

They're singing at us

Tarts!

WHALES song…

DONNIE BLACK
Siren song!
Cover your ears lads!
They'll make you forget your wives back home

ALL but DONNIE MAC cover their ears.

DONNIE MAC
Fine by me!

WHALES song…

COXN/DONNIE BLACK
Dive on

The list of Russian submariners sleepily takes us into…

SONAR
Unidentified noise sir…

THE BOSS
Yes?

SONAR
Still unidentified sir.

THE BOSS
Find it.

DONNIE BLACK
'then silence, like a poultice, comes,
to heals the blows of sound'…

    BOSS looks at DONNIE BLACK.

Poetry, sir.
Finding patterns of meaning

THE BOSS
Finding fucking *noise*, Coxn

THE BOSS
Navigator Captain. Suggested course and speed?

NAVIGATOR/VOICE OVER
270 speed 4 depth 80 m sir. – and happy with that sir.

SONAR/VOICE OVER
Ops Sonar controller

OPS/VOICE OVER
 Ops

SONAR/VOICE OVER
Standby for contact brief.

OPS/VOICE OVER
OPs: Standing by.

SONAR/VOICE OVER
Sonar controller: Three contacts held on sonar. First contact
contact 001 bearing green or red 90 centre bearing 180 or 000
faint tonal contact in two beams. Possible submarine contact

need to resolve bearing. Broadband contact, Contact 002 bearing red 50 centre bearing 220 in out, cavitation, whine audible, classification possible warship. Investigating. Final sonar contact broadband contact 003 bearing red 110 centre bearing 130 faint cavitation in out whine audible possible warship investigating.

OPS
Ops roger…

As…

ELEVEN – BUNKS

CASANOVAKEN and NEWDADMIKE in bunks.

CASANOVA is masturbating…

CASANOVA
Maria get hold of me yes with your mouth…there…

NEWDADMIKE
Ken!

Keep it down will you mate?

CASANOVAKEN
Sorry, Mate.

NEWDADMIKE
Take it out of the Sleeping Area, will you?

CASANOVAKEN
Yes mate. Sorry mate.

Gets out, goes to HEADS as…

SONAR
This is Sonar.
This is DJ Sonar Spooky of
Marginal Ice Zone's most popular and only radio station…

It's midnight

It's always midnight under water

This is DJ Sonar

Playing your favourite sea tracks…

At number four…

Ice floes colliding

> *And we hear them…*

At number three…

Seals

> *And we hear them…*

At number two/

Killer whales

> *And we hear it…*

And at number one…

Snow

> *And, delicately, this too…*

It's snowing up there…

> *Also…*

> *Also…*

DONNIE BLACK
(*Reading…*) 'Haiku are epigrammatic nature poems in which the writer aims to achieve maximum effect by minimum means…the best haiku are allusive and oblique yet piercingly clear…comprised usually of 15-17 syllables…

eg

Silent flowers
Speak also
To that obedient ear within'

> *He counts the number of syllables…*

(*Silently mouths..*) si lent flow ers speak al so to that o be di ent ear wi thin…

16…

> *Makes up…*

Submariners
talk cobblers
To my   wax-filled cauliflower ear …/

(*Counts…*) sub mar in ers talk cob lers to my wax filled col I
flow er ear

17!

> *He's rather pleased with himself.*

> *Also…*

RADIO OPERATOR/DONNIE MAC
Listening intently to…
*RUSSIAN radio conversations between 'The Peter The Great', The
Karelia, The Kursk…*
He has a Russian phrasebook [tourist-style]

(*Russian…*) spa-koy-nee no chi, Russian naval fleet…

Naval fleet…(*looks it up…*) 'uoctb'…boehhom opckoro…

(*Hears… Russian for …*) 'pycckorro dcnota'

> *Looks it up.*

That's…peter the great…flagship…

'Kursk' (*Looks it up…*) nothing…

what's 'Kursk'

Kursk

TWELVE – FAMILYGRAMS [TWO]

Everybody eating…normal utensils…

DONNIE MAC enters with…

DONNIE MAC
It's that time again!

Four weeks!

Familygrams!

> *Gives them out to DONNIE BLACK, CASANOVA, himself…*

> *To dolls…*

Nothing for you Ivan Ivan Ivan Ivan Ivan Ivan Ivan and Igor
You have to understand, boys…*nobody* loves you Soviets…

DONNIE BLACK
Russians they're *Russians* now *not Soviets*

NEWDADMIKE
Don't do this again.

DONNIE MAC
Not doing it again, mate.
Wasn't one for you.

DONNIE BLACK
Give it a rest mate…

DONNIE MAC
No, honest…not arsing about this time…
There really isn't one for you, Mike mate, honest, sorry.

> *NEWDADMIKE heads for RADIO ROOM…*

NEWDADMIKE
I'm warning you, mate…

CASANOVA
Don't mess with a New Dad, mate…

> *DONNIE MAC puts NEWDAD's Familygram in his place.*

DONNIE BLACK
You mean bastard

> *NEWDADMIKE arrives back…*

NEWDADMIKE
You lying fucking lying/mean bastard!

DONNIE MAC
It's right there you blind bastard

NEWDADMIKE
You bastard.
Not funny.

DONNIE MAC
You're such a gullible bastard
You know that 'gullible' doesn't appear in *any* dictionary?

NEWDADMIKE
Yes it does…it…/oh fuck…not funny

DONNIE MAC
Very funny.

CASANOVAKEN
Can we just read what we've got in *peace*????

TWO DONNIES
Oooooooooh can we hear from Diarrh/oea

CASANOVAKEN
Maria!!!
MARIA!!!
Alright????

TWO DONNIES
Ooooh!!!

    And they read…

    They read little grams containing the following…

MARIA
Went clubbing. Wore gold lame dress in memory of you. Been
playing with puppies all night. They really missing the things
you teach them. Pussy and I lying on my bed both missing
you. Pets missing your petting. Love you. Maria

MRS MAC
Whole house running like clockwork. Roy now attacking
garden. Took out the old apple tree. Replanted your rockery
with alpines. Has rationalised your shed for you and painted it
leftover yellow. Still not charging! Giving him his breakfast in
lieu. Deb.

MICHELLE
Madison loves new pram. Went to park yesterday. Mum and Dad here again. Cant keep away from granddaughter. Gareth took new photos of Madison in pink frock from your Sarah. Love you. Miss you. Big kiss from us.

MRS BLACK
All well here. MOT cost bomb. You owe me. On patio with glass wine reading poem I found in underwear drawer you wrote to me. You Big Softie. I love you.

DONNIE BLACK
(*Its perfect.*) She's on the patio with the pinot grigio

DONNIE MAC
She's let him paint my fucking *shed*!

CASANOVAKEN
Gold strapless dress. Sweet Jesus!

Heads for BUNKS.

NEWDADMIKE
She's been out in her pram.
Park.
Must be sunny at home.

Heads for BUNKS.

DONNIE MAC
Fucking warm *yellow!*

As…

THIRTEEN – UNDER THE POLAR ICE CAP

Everybody in various parts of the boat…

THE BOSS
Coxon take the submarine to diving stations

COXN
Take the submarine to diving stations aye aye sir

On main broadcast.

Diving stations

Presses general alarm three times.

Diving stations diving stations

DCHQ/VOICE OVER
close up all reports to DCHQ

Pause while people close up at their stations.

THE BOSS
(*To NAVIGATOR.*) What's our position?

NAVIGATOR/CASANOVAKEN
At the north pole, sir.
wow
how amazing is this

TWO DONNIES
(*Winding up…*) wow
how amazing is this!

NAVIGATOR/KEN
Ready in all respects to break through.
Upward sounding indicates thin ice above.

THE BOSS
(*He thinks…*) Ice is…

Okay

No problem…

OK Cox'n we can just drive up.

Navigator – Depth of water to ice?

NAVIGATOR/KEN
38m sir

THE BOSS
Roger. Cox'n 6 up

COXN/DONNIE BLACK
6 up

Repeats to PLANESMAN.

6 up

To SYS CON OPERATOR.

Pump 500 litres from Ms and Os to sea.

PLANESMAN/NEWDADMIKE
6 up achieved

SYSCON
Pumping.

NAVIGATOR
(*Calls out the depth between top of fin and bottom of the ice in 3m increments…*) 36m

This would be quite slow between each depth reading.

33m

30m

27m

24m

As…

DONNIE MAC
(*To CASANOVA.*) Look at the icicles!
Bet you wish Diesel Maria/could see these great big white long *things*

CASANOVA
She's not called 'Diesel Maria' She's just *Maria* and I just said she said she *liked* the smell of diesel…

DONNIE MAC
She'll have only ever seen a tiny little white short thing…

COXN/DONNIE BLACK
Finished pumping from Ms; pumping from Os

THE BOSS
Navigator inform me when the sounding reaches 20m

NAVIGATOR/KEN
Roger sir, 20m
Captain sir sounding 20m

THE BOSS
Captain roger. Stop engines

COXN/DONNIE BLACK
Stop engines roger sir

> *Leans forward and moves the engine telegraph to 'stop' – it makes a clunking sound as he turns it; but instantaneously Manoeuvre Room would repeat it and a buzzer sounds out of the console in front as...*

Ice Lovers...

we are at the absolute North Pole

Five months early but...Happy Christmas, everybody!

CASANOVAKEN
(*Cheers and...*) *Singing:* 'Jack Frost roasting on an open fire... Chestnuts nipping at your nose...'

DONNIE MAC
Look Ma...top of the world!

DONNIE BLACK
Engine telegraph repeats stopped sir

THE BOSS
Roger telegraph

> *The propeller shaft will stop during this.*

NAVIGATOR/KEN
10m

THE BOSS
Cox'n make a pipe about to break through.

COXN/DONNIE BLACK
Roger sir, make a pipe about to break through.
(*On broadcast.*) Do you hear there cox'n speaking about to break through the ice – standby for contact.

finished pumping hull valve shut.

NAVIGATOR/KEN
6m – resolution lost on the echo sounder.

THE BOSS
Captain roger 6m. Switch off echo sounder.

NAVIGATOR/KEN
Roger switch off echo sounder, switched off.

>   *BOSS feels they are about to break through.*

THE BOSS
Indicated speed and keel depth?

COXN/DONNIE BLACK
1 knot – and 17m sir.

THE BOSS
Roger

>   *SILENCE waiting for the contact to happen…*

>   *Waiting for a rasping sound at slow speed.*

THE BOSS
Cox'n keel depth?

COXN/DONNIEBLACK
Keel depth is 13m (…*that is with 7m of the fin out of the ice…*)

>   *BOSS gets them to put some air in ballast to hold the sub still against*
>   *the ice.*

THE BOSS
put a one second blow in number 1 and 4 main ballast tanks

SYS/DONNIE BLACK
Roger sir put a one second blow in number 1 and 4 main
ballast tanks

>   *Leans forward and operates two toggle switches on the console for*
>   *one and four main ballast tanks blows.*

THE BOSS
Raise ECM mast one all round sweep and report

SYS/DONNIE BLACK
Roger sir raise ECM mast

Raises mast with switch.

ECM mast fully raised.

OPS/DONNIE MAC
Captain sir one all round sweep no contacts.

THE BOSS
Roger lower ECM mast

SYS/DONNIE BLACK
Roger lower ECM mast. ECM mast fully lowered.

THE BOSS
Raise search till I say well

SYS/DONNIE BLACK
Roger sir, raise search till you say well

Looks over his right shoulder as he does it.

THE BOSS
Well. It's pure white
pure white serene ice all around us

ALL
Oooh!

THE BOSS
(*Turns periscope eastwards.*) There's a rainbow

ALL
Oooh!

THE BOSS
It looks like its made of millions of multi-shade diamonds

COXN/DONNIEBLACK
Very good use of (*New word.*) alliteration, sir…

M's d's

NEWDADMIKE
Will we be getting out, sir?

Walk about a bit?
Build a snowman?

THE BOSS
Afraid not Mike.
How can we get out and walk about a bit if we're not actually here?

NEWDADMIKE
Didn't think of that sir.

THE BOSS
I do the thinking.
That's why I'm the Commanding Officer, son

> *BOSS does a sweep around at the end of the first sweep because he's happy he says…*

Raise WT mast (*Wireless mast.*)

> *This continues under…*

SYS/DONNIE BLACK
Roger sir raise WT – WT going up

OPS
WT OPs

WT/DONNIE MAC
WT

OPS
WT mast going up

WT/DONNIE MAC
WT roger.

> *This means transmission can be received…*

CASANOVAKEN
We're not going out?

NEWDADMIKE
No

We're not here.

ALL
Awwwwwwww!

DONNIE BLACK
Bugger that.
Eskimo suits on!

>   *They pretend to put on Eskimo clothes.*

Do your fur buttons up
It's cold out there…

>   *They all obey. Fur buttons are quite fiddly…*

Okay…
Out we go

>   *They all step out onto pretend ice, all over the boat…*

Okay…
Careful on the ice boys…
Might be slippy…

>   *It might be…*

>   *Once upright…*

ALL
Wow

>   *Stare amazed.*

>   *It is very quiet.*

>   *Very awe-inspiring.*

>   *Until…*

DONNIE BLACK
Feel the terrific ice silence

ALL
Wow

DONNIE BLACK
See the splendour

ALL
What splendour!

DONNIE BLACK
Collect memories with your cameras, lads.
Take them back to those you've left at home far far away.

They all pretend to take pictures.

Make the noise of busy camera shutters.

CASANOVA
Penguin

DONNIEMAC
Polar bear

Glacier

DONNIE BLACK
Father Christmas!

Elves!

CASANOVA
Maria   in white fur bikini

ALL
Maria in white fur bikini

Very busy camera shutters.

THE BOSS
What's happening?

COXN/DONNIE BLACK
The men are all out on the North pole taking photo
memories sir

They're

THE BOSS
Bonkers.

Absolutely Bonkers.

Hope you're all wearing sunscreen out there...?

MEN
And sunglasses. Yes sir.

THE BOSS
Very wise.

Mast stops with sys operating switch.

Cox'n fall out from diving stations go to the watch

COXN/DONNIE BLACK
Fall out from diving stations go to the watch, roger sir
(*On broadcast:*) Do you hear there fall out from diving stations,
go to the watch. First watch. Watch dived. Patrol quiet state.

THE BOSS
Now we've got our head out of the water…
Let's see what our really clean ears can pick up…

As the machinery gathers information…

Incoming sounds…

FOURTEEN – A SMALL DEATH

Captain's cabin.

DONNIE MAC brings something…

RADIO OP/DONNIE MAC
Sir.
Something you should see I think.

And delivers a message…

THE BOSS
Oh dear. Oh dear.

Cot Death.

Madison Emily Hannah

Oh the poor bloody man.

RADIO OP/DONNIE MAC
Yes sir.

Tough one, sir.

THE BOSS
When do we tell him?

Do we tell him?

We've three weeks to go…

We can't get him off yet…no chance

RADIO OP/DONNIE MAC
No Sir

THE BOSS
We're too covert…we're too bloody far from anything
NATO…

RADIO OP/DONNIE MAC
Yes Sir

THE BOSS
What does it say on his brief…?
Was she poorly before he left…
I mean…will he have any idea…?

DONNIE MAC
Been talking like everything's perfect, sir…

THE BOSS
Will he be wondering…?
What does it say?
Does he want to be told about Bad News?

RADIO OP/DONNIE MAC
Not till last day out, sir

THE BOSS
Poor bloody family

Do we tell him?

RADIO OP/DONNIE MAC
Don't know sir.

Your call.

THE BOSS
Yes. My call.
Poor Mike.

Shit.

> *He thinks.*

I think we keep this between you and me.

RADIO OP/DONNIE MAC
Yes sir.

THE BOSS
Leave it with me.
shit.
Keep it between the two us.

RADIO OP/DONNIE MAC
Yes sir.
It's familygram time sir…shall I…

THE BOSS
Well, deliver them as normal
Let's keep *some* men happy…

FIFTEEN – FAMILY GRAMS [THREE]

> *They are all sat, crammed very close, watching Notting Hill.*

> *They are all eating a choc ice.*

> *Apart from the Russian dolls, who are watching impassively.*

ALL
(…*along with Julia Roberts…who has just been turned down by Hugh Grant…*) 'Fine.
Fine.
Good decision.'

DONNIE BLACK
You plonker Hugh Grant…
She's *Julia Roberts!*

ALL
'the *fame* thing isn't really real, you know.

And don't forget
I'm also just a *girl*
Standing in front of a boy
Asking him to love her…'

DONNIE BLACK
(*To NEWDADMIKE.*) You crying, Newdad?

Why you crying New Daddy?

NEWDADMIKE
Don't know. Sorry Mate.
Emotion. Build-up Thing.

DONNIE BLACK
(*Gives him a hug…*) New Daddy!
you Big Girl,

> *DONNIE MAC enters with…*

DONNIE MAC
Familygrams!

> *Gives them out to DONNIE BLACK, CASANOVA, himself…*

DONNIE BLACK
(*To dolls… And, yet again.*) Igor…tell the Ivans…sorry…again…
Nothing for Russia…
You're just not *popular* …

NEWDADMIKE
Don't do this again.

DONNIE MAC
Not doing it again, mate.
Wasn't one for you.

DONNIE BLACK
Give it a rest mate…

DONNIE MAC
No, honest…not arsing about this time…
There really isn't one for you, Mike mate, honest, sorry.

NEWDADMIKE heads for RADIO ROOM…

NEWDADMIKE
I'm warning you, mate…
You lying fucking lying bastard where is it?

DONNIE MAC
I'm sorry, mate. I'm really not kidding.

NEWDADMIKE
Lying bastard!

He grabs DONNIE MAC, starts searching him…

CASANOVA
Woa, Sunshine…take it easy.

DONNIE MAC
I'm sorry Mate, I'm really sorry.

DONNIE BLACK
Let's all calm down, shall we?
Donnie Mac…
There's really not one for him?

DONNIEMAC
Really not.
Really not.

TWO DONNIES exchange a look. Minimal.

DONNIEBLACK
Okay.
Sometimes stuff just doesn't come through.
No big deal.
Just need to be patient.
Look at the Russians…
You'll never see Ivan Ivan Ivan Ivan Ivan Ivan Ivan and Igor
losing it…
Practise that icy Soviet calm…

He starts the film again…

NEWDADMIKE
(*To DONNIE MAC…*) Sorry mate. Emotional Build-up Thing.

DONNIE MAC
Ah, fuck, mate.
Pressure.
Forget it.
Watch the film…

CASANOVAKEN
(*To Julia…*) after all Julia…I'm just a submariner, wanting a girl
to love him!

> *They are very crammed together.*

> *DONNIE MAC puts an awkward arm round NEWDADMIKE.*

NEWDADMIKE
Fuck!

> *They watch or pretend to watch, the movie.*

SIXTEEN – AN ABNORMAL AMOUNT OF DATA

> *All gathered, mess, for briefing…*

THE BOSS
Gentlemen
We're monitoring the Russian Federations Naval Exercise
In The Barents.
The exercise has *Chinese* Observers
Which is getting NATO a bit hot under the collar.
Or primary task is an underwater look on
Their latest 10 Oscar 11 class nuclear attack submarine
Which Vasco will now
Brief you on…
Navigator

NAVIGATOR/KEN
Captain. Sir.

> *BOSS sits.*

> *NAVIGATOR stands.*

> *CASANOVAKEN is a bit new to this…*

Very, very subtly, other CREW demonstrate this…

First. Environmental.

   Chart.

We're approaching from a north easterly direction
Contact with the Russian fleet is imminent.
Relatively shallow sea at 200-250 metres.
There is a layer at around 80metres so we'll be taking
Regular bathy shots…
Our Safe depth will be 60 metres throughout.
Weather is fair to moderate
Slight swell of 2 to 4 metres
Therefore visibility from the air will be good.

ALL
(*Almost sotto voce but…*) Whoops!

NAVIGATOR/KEN
(*Chart.*) Shipping is low to moderate.
Two main shipping lanes…see chart.
Possible threats.

Our last available intelligence
Confirmed the presence of…

   Photograph.

Aircraft Carrier probably *Peter the Great.*

Main threat. Active sonar. And helicopters.

ALL
(*Mouth…*) Shit

CASANOVAKEN
Also
The *Boriso-Glebsk*
The *Danii Moskovsky*
Delta 1V ballistic missile S/M *Karelia*

   Photographs…

Awaiting details on these…fortunately…
They're still a long way south west…

Most important for *us*

> *Photograph.*

Oscar 11-class Submarine
Aka
Kursk
Length 154 meters draught 32 metres, beam 18 meters, a
dived speed of 28kts maximum diving depth of 600 metres
She has a double hull the outer made from austenistic steel a
third of an inch thick which has a lower magnetic signature…
which is a bastard to track through the water…
And she's covered in rubber

DONNIE MAC
Trollope

NAVIGATOR KEN
Displacement of 18,000 tons.
Propulsion 2 shafts, 7 blades average RPM 50-100
Powered by nuclear reactor

THE BOSS
Remember her in The Med in 1999, Coxn?

DONNIE BLACK
She can do 28 knots submerged so…

THE BOSS
She's not *quite* as fast as us…

> *Others put thumbs up…*

Interesting fact…
She's capable of unleashing more destructive power than was
used in the entire 2nd World War.

NEW DAD MIKE
Thanks for that, sir

THE BOSS
Carry on Navigator

NAVIGATOR/KEN
Main threat.

24GRANIT Nuclear missiles each with independent
warheads, automatic guidance systems
intelligence tells us one of these being test fired in this exercise.
Intelligence want a close look.
Also packing SHKVAL weapons
And HTP torpedoes.

DONNIE BLACK
HTP? That's bloody dangerous…

DONNIE MAC
Bloody dangerous as opposed to 24 nuclear missiles?

CASANOVA
Moving on…

DONNIE BLACK
Hydrogen peroxide…

…HTP's fucking unstable when it mixes with oil or water……

CASANOVAKEN
Moving on…

DONNIE BLACK
We dropped them in 1950/
Bad idea.

THE BOSS
Coxn.
History lesson some other time…

DONNIE BLACK
Yes sir.

NAVIGATOR/KEN
Kursk also has a modern Towed Array Sonar…

ALL groan.

Blue threat.
Two Los Angeles Class SSN's operating in the area/
The Memphis
And
The Toledo

ALL
(*Sotto voce Hum…*) 'O say can you see
By the dawn's early light
What so proudly we…
At the twilight's last gleaming…

NAVIGATOR/KEN
We need to be in and out and quickly as possible.

Ultra quiet state.

Captain

THE BOSS
Navigator. Thank you.
Okay.
Kursk.
Let's go capture her on celluloid…
The sub for the 21st Century…
In all her radiant beauty.

> *Everyone to stations as…*

> *NEWDADMIKE goes to…*

SEVENTEEN – A LOOK THROUGH THE WINDOW

> *Periscope…THE BOSS there…*

NEWDADMIKE
Sir.

THE BOSS
Mike

NEWDADMIKE
Can I have a look through the window, sir?

THE BOSS
Sure.

> *He lets him look through as…*

NEWDADMIKE
Thanks, sir.

THE BOSS
Well over halfway through mission, Mike.

NEWDADMIKE
Yes sir.

THE BOSS
Missing home?

NEWDADMIKE
New baby.

THE BOSS
Ah.

All a bit much, having to leave…someone…new…
Photo?

    NEWDADMIKE shows him a photograph…

Name?

NEWDADMIKE
Madison
Madison Emily Hannah

THE BOSS
Unusual name…

NEWDADMIKE
Wife's choice

    NEWDADMIKE does 'women!' look.

THE BOSS
She's very pretty.

NEWDADMIKE
She takes after the wife.

    Pause.

THE BOSS
Well, you don't want her taking after an ugly bugger like you, do you?

Gives photo back.

One more look out the window?

NEWDADMIKE
Thank you, Sir.

He looks through the periscope.

Sunny back home apparently.
Wife had to get a sun-canopy for the pram…

THE BOSS
Did she?

NEWDADMIKE
Thank you sir.

NEWDADMIKE leaves.

Still bleeding wet here.

And *bloody.*

And he looks through the periscope.

EIGHTEEN – UNDERWATER LOOK

DONNIE MAC
Ops sonar controller contact 001 bearing 179 tonals stronger

OPS/KEN
Roger

DONNIE MAC
Ops sonar controller

KEN
Ops

DONNIE MAC
Faint broadband on the bearing of contact 001, bearing 176, faint whine audible, tonals stronger, contact possibly moving left…

THE BOSS
Sonar controller captain

DONNIE MAC
Sonar controller sir.

THE BOSS
We are moving into position for underwater look of master contact 001 Oscar II class submarine.

DONNIE MAC
Sound room roger, sir.

THE BOSS
Cox'n pipe watch stand to. underwater look of Oscar II class submarine.
Assume ultra quiet state

COXN/DONNIEBLACK
(*On fwd broadcast.*) Roger sir. (*Into mic.*) watch stand to underwater look. Assume ultra quiet state

> *All non-essentials to bunks. Limited movements. Ventilation stopped. Showers switched off. Water isolated. Galley shut down. People speak in lowered voices in the control room. SYS CON switches various buttons to shut down areas of the boat.*

COXN/DONNIE BLACK
OK lads, low sexy voices
Move like butterflies sting like bees…

> *Very very quiet voices…stealth as…*

THE BOSS
Ops course and speed

OPS/KEN
001 course and speed 175 speed 4

THE BOSS
Roger. 3 down keep 100m revolutions for 5 knots.

COXN/DONNIE BLACK
3 down keep 100m revolutions for 5 knots aye aye sir

PLANESMAN/NEWDADMIKE
3 down keep 100m

> *COXN winds on revs for five knots.*

COXN/DONNIE BLACK
Captain sir cox'n

THE BOSS
Captain

COXN/DONNIE BLACK
watch stood to sir.

THE BOSS
roger raise search until I say well.

SYS/DONNIE BLACK
Raise search until you say well, roger sir, search going up

> *Looks over right shoulder.*

THE BOSS
Well! Raise monitor underwater camera to same level

SYS/DONNIE BLACK
Raise monitor underwater camera to same level, roger sir

> *Switches to operate periscope going up.*

SONAR/DONNIE MAC
Sonar controller, Ops.

OPS/KEN
Ops

SONAR/DONNIE MAC
Strong broadband contact with contact 001 classified as Oscar II nuclear submarine K141…

DONNIEBLACK
Kursk

SONAR/DONNIE MAC
…now showing in twenty degrees of bow sonar.

THE BOSS
Roger lined up and ready to start on run.
All positions start watches and recorders.

Watches set, recorders on…

OPS/KEN
Datum marked sir

SONAR/DONNIE MAC
Target strength increasing. Now shows in 6 beams.

THE BOSS
Master contact 001

SONAR/DONNIE MAC
Roger sir, designate master contact 001.

OPS/KEN
Ops captain. Range approximately 1800 metres.

THE BOSS
Roger. We are going in closer.

Everyone is even stiller…

Sonar, captain. Give bearing reports until I say well.

SONAR/DONNIE MAC
Roger. Give bearing reports until you say well.
176

THE BOSS
800 metres

SONAR/DONNIE MAC
175

THE BOSS
600 metres

SONAR/DONNIE MAC
175

THE BOSS
400 metres

SONAR/DONNIE MAC
174

THE BOSS
200 metres. Well.

Underneath propellers.

> *Silence on board except for the click of cameras – operated by THE BOSS from a button on his periscope.*

> *Everybody almost turns to see the huge Kursk above them.*

> *Sound of propellers.*

> *A huge object passing overhead.*

> *ALL mouth 'fuck' in wonderment.*

Underneath Keel.

Ops, captain. Reload film.

OPS/KEN
Roger sir, film reload in process.

> *Some slight activity before.*

Film reloaded

> *More pictures.*

THE BOSS
Clear of the bow

> *The CO turns his periscope round and follows the bow until it is no longer visible.*

Clear water. Excellent view. Bow still visible.

What a Big Girl!

THE BOSS
Down search.

SYS/DONNIE BLACK
Lower search roger sir (*Looks over shoulder.*)

THE BOSS
Sound room are we still in broadband contact?

SONAR/DONNIE MAC
Just faded sir

THE BOSS
Roger starboard 15 steer 300

COXN/DONNIE BLACK
Starboard 15 sir steer 300

PLANESMAN/NEWDADMIKE
starboard 15 steer 300. 15 of starboard wheel on.

THE BOSS
2 up keep 60m revolutions for 10 knots.

COXN/DONNIE BLACK
2 up keep 60m revolutions for 10 knots aye aye sir

> *Leans forward and winds on the revs. Pause.*

Captain sir on course 300 on depth 60m speed 10 knots

> *CASANOVAKEN moves from his station towards aft…*

CASANOVA/KEN
Heads Coxn. Urgent.

> *All still in ultra quiet state.*

THE BOSS
Very good.

She's apparently got a relaxation area

COXN/DONNIE BLACK
I say

THE BOSS
And an aquarium.

COXN/DONNIE BLACK
Aquarium?

In a sub????

The Russians are *mad!*

THE BOSS
Bonkers…And a sauna

COXN/DONNIE BLACK
(*Austin Powers.*) Yeah Baby! Sir.

Shall we ask if they want to swap, Sir?

THE BOSS
Unfaithful talk

COXN/DONNIE BLACK
Very deeply ashamed, sir.

> *The rhythmic clicking noise starts up…*

THE BOSS
That bloody noise again!!!

Find that bloody noise!!!!

DONNIE MAC/NEWDADMIKE
Yes sir!

THE BOSS
Noise Husbandry routine
For fuck's sake!!!

> *And DONNIE MAC and NEWDADMIKE are very near THE HEADS…*

DONNIE MAC
It's in *this* vicinity

NEWDADMIKE
Shhh!

> *They listen.*

THE BOSS
And get some clear water between us and that oversized
Russian bastard!

NEWDADMIKE
It's coming from The Heads…

Is it plumbing or something…?

Sounds like…metal though, doesn't it…?

DONNIE MAC
Shhh!

> *They creep up…gingerly open the door…*
>
> *Where CASANOVAKEN is sitting with masturbatory equipment…*
>
> *Wanking…his big watch clinking against the pipes…*

Bloody Casanova!

CASANOVA
For fuck sake…can't a man follow Manly Pursuits???

DONNIE MAC
Not in *ultra quiet state!*

Not in his bloody *wristwatch!!!*

We've located the unusual and worrying sound, coxon!

Casanova wanking in his *wristwatch*!!!

COXN/DONNIE BLACK
Very poor.
He'll have to suffer for that.
Wristwatch!
Plonker!

NINETEEN – THE KURSK LIGHTS THE FUSE

And a small explosion is heard, far far away…

SONAR/VOICE OVER
Ops sonar controller

OPS/KEN
Ops

SONAR/VOICE OVER
Loud Bang heard edge of the starboard beam, sounded metallic, possible explosion.

OPS/KEN
Ops roger; ops captain sir

THE BOSS
Captain

OPS/KEN
sonar reports bang heard on sonar – edge of the starboard beam possible explosion.

THE BOSS
Roger,
Is that the bearing of Kursk?

OPS/KEN
One faint narrowband tonal contact suggests from bearing of the target of under water look: Oscar II class submarine. Kursk.

THE BOSS
Ops are you saying the bang came from Kursk?

COXN/DONNIE BLACK
Did somebody hit her????

OPS/KEN
Seems likely, Captain.
Waiting for Sound Room to confirm.

THE BOSS
Cox'n captain – starboard 10 steer three four zero.

COXN/DONNIE BLACK
Roger sir, starboard 10 steer three four zero.
(*To PLANESMAN...*) starboard 10 steer 340

>   *There is a HUGE HUGE BANG.*

>   *Everyone jars to the left.*

SONAR/DONNIE MAC
(*Shouts.*) sonar blanked! (*This means the ship is blind.*)

COXN
Emergency stations
(*Pushes general alarm button 3x.*) Emergency stations. Emergency stations.
Loud unexplained bang external to the submarine. DCHQ close up. All compartments conduct phase one damage control checks and report to DCHQ.

PLANESMAN
Off depth by 10m – regaining depth!

   He calls out the metre depth readings as…

67

64

61

on depth 60 (*See lower down.*)

THE BOSS
Start event 003 Annotate all records (*On broadcast. Starts stopwatch.*)

   Now a jumble of voices comes in:

RATING/VOICE OVER
(*On broadcast.*) Control room 29 bulkhead.

COXN/DONNIE BLACK
Ship control

RATING/VOICE OVER
(*On broadcast.*) have an injury in the fwd port bunk space. Need medical assistance

COX/DONNIE BLACK
Roger. Pass to DCHQ.

MANOEUVRE ROOM/VOICE OVER
(*Talking to someone in the engine room unaware that he's on main broadcast.*) Lower level OK will get medical assistance as soon as possible (*On broadcast.*)

ENGINE ROOM/VOICE OVER
Think it's a fucking broken leg. Chalky's *screaming* Nobby…don't *move* him! Fucking Hurry up!!!

COX/DONNIE BLACK
Manoeuvring ship control you're on main broadcast.

MANOEUVRE ROOM/VOICE OVER
Roger ship control.

Click of switch sound as MR takes itself off main broadcast.

THE BOSS
DCHQ captain. Report.

DCHQ/VOICE OVER
Captain DCHQ – phase one reports complete. Valve leaking on after trim tank. Not serious. Isolated and effecting a repair. Some broken lights. Senior 8 injured by flying broken crockery in mess. Laceration. Two further reported injuries. One in port fwd bunkspace – sprained wrist and slight head injury – and one in the lower level of the engine room. Broken leg or badly twisted knee. Medical parties proceeding to casualties.

SYS CON immediately refers to his TAB which is a training aid book. A5 in size. Diagrammatic reference of the circuit that has been isolated. He is assessing what this means for him should he need to use it, now that part of the system is isolated.

THE BOSS
Captain roger. Keep me informed. Sound room captain

SONAR/DONNIE MAC
Sonar controller

THE BOSS
Any more information on the direction of the explosion?

PLANESMAN/NEWDADMIKE
61

COXN/DONNIE BLACK
ON depth 60m – captain sir I have the bubble

> *Which means the COXN is happy with ship control everything is working.*

Captain sir ship control

THE BOSS
Captain

COXN/DONNIE BLACK
Permission to test planes and rudder.

THE BOSS
Yes please.

COXN/DONNIE BLACK
(*Turns to planesman.*) check the planes check the rudder

PLANESMAN/NEWDADMIKE
roger check planes and rudder.

> *Pushes stick forward and left and right etc.*

Planes and rudder following!

COXN/DONNIE BLACK
Captain sir ship control. Happy with the planes and steering.

THE BOSS
Roger. Carry on planing keep 60m steer 340.

COX/DONNIE BLACK
Roger sir carry on planing keep 60m steer 340.

THE BOSS
Sound room what's happening?

SONAR/DONNIE MAC
Captain sir contact's engine noise ceased; compressed cavitation ceased. Sounds as if it's going down. We have lost tonal contact. Bearing is approximately 125 – we are hearing

breaking up noises. Metallic noises and hull popping. Piping
through…

> *And everybody listens as…*

> *They hear…*

> *Creaking metallic noises.*

THE BOSS
She's lost propulsion

> *Bubbles.*

> *Further bangs (not explosions).*

COXN/DONNIE BLACK
She's on her way down…

> *We hear THE KURSK in her death throes…*

> *Groaning.*

> *Possible compressed cavitation.*

> *Gurgling.*

> *Eerie/echo type background noise.*

> *Other vessels.*

> *Then…*

PLANESMAN/NEWDADMIKE
She's hit the seab/ed…

> *Silence almost…*

THE BOSS
Listen!!!

> *Now no sound…*

Jesus Christ!

> *He consults his stopwatch.*

Time from first explosion to seabed…
135 seconds

Jesus Christ!

Jesus Christ!

Everybody watches him…

Finally…

Sound room captain.

SONAR/DONNIE MAC
Sound room

THE BOSS
Confirm that you were holding the tonal before the event
started and that you have lost it now.

SONAR/DONNIE MAC
Standby.

Everybody waits…

Captain sir, sonar controller

THE BOSS
Captain

SONAR/DONNIE MAC
Can confirm tonal no longer held

THE BOSS
Roger.
They've lost her.

The bloody Kursk the submarine for the 21st century
Lost her…

He's not thinking…

COXN
Sir…

Perhaps clear the area…

Perhaps go to safe distance…
In case in case we're in for a nuclear disaster…

THE BOSS
Christ…*yes!*

COXN/DONNIE BLACK
Perhaps get to periscope depth…
Intercept signal traffic…see if we can find out what's going on…?

If we can help…?   at all

THE BOSS
Mono*maniacal* confidence

COXN/DONNIE BLACK
Yes, sir.

THE BOSS
Here we are
Here we go

TWENTY – NEWS FROM OUTSIDE

THE BOSS heads for his cabin, men regroup about the boat.

The air becomes very busy with radio messages between the Russian Navy, incoming reports to NAVAL COMMAND at Northwood… offers of assistance from a variety of nations.

And then…a progression of Russian official announcements…moving from 'there is absolutely nothing wrong'…to… 'there may be a slight problem' to 'there is a big problem, but we are dealing with it'.

TWENTY ONE – REPLAYING THE SOUNDTRACK, LOOKING AT THE PICTURES

THE BOSS and SONAR listening…also with charts, data, photos of the KURSK…

Everything is being studied minutely.

SONAR/DONNIE MAC
This is what we got…

Sonar operators replaying mystery blasts through low-frequency analyser…

They listen intently…

Is that something *hitting* her…????

THE BOSS
It's…an *immediate* explosion…quite small…
Again…

First explosion…

SONAR/DONNIE MAC
It sounds *internal* forward…

THE BOSS
I think that's something going wrong with the torpedo
launch…

SONAR/DONNIE MAC
Something jammed or blew or something…

THE BOSS
Some lazy Soviet bastard hasn't kept their torpedo room spic
and span…something's fucked up and…(*Bang.*)
you men might take a lesson from this why I am
always banging on about Deep Cleaning!!!!

SONAR/DONNIE MAC
Yes sir.

THE BOSS
And *rigour*

SONAR/DONNIE MAC
Yes sir.
Listen again?

They listen on…

It is torture to hear…

THE BOSS
Why didn't they open her valves
Bring her up???

SONAR/DONNIE MAC
No time probably…

That bang's probably taken out the control room as well as the Bomb Room so…nobody alive there to…steer the boat…

THE BOSS
Christ

SONAR/DONNIE MAC
Listen…sir…

She's out of control…
She travels a quarter of a mile…
Descends 107 metres…
She's…it's not *deep* there…

THE BOSS
The warheads…
They'd just be cooking
Then…

SONAR/DONNIE MAC
The whole Bomb shop goes up.

THE BOSS
Jesus Christ!

> *We hear the loudest explosion again.*
>
> *The Kursk hitting the seabed and…*

SONAR/DONNIE MAC
Something's contained it sir…
otherwise…
explosion of that much fire power sir…
we'd all be in the shit, sir

THE BOSS
That's true.

SONAR/DONNIEMAC
Sir, listen to this…

> *A sound of rhythmical tapping…*

I picked this up half an hour ago…

If the explosion didn't go completely *aft*…
That sound…

THE BOSS
Is somebody alive……

SONAR/DONNIE MAC
If her construction has contained the blast…
That's men asking for help, sir…

Silence.

Can we respond sir?

Can we offer assistance?

THE BOSS
Let me think…

They both look at their watches…

DONNIEMAC
Their emergency air…bit limited sir…no light no heat /sir…

THE BOSS
I know!
I know…
But
We're an *attack* vessel
Not a fucking *lifeboat*!!!
Let me think if we can actually respond.
Let me think…make a decision…

Watch again…

Okay… Almost four oclockers …okay…
Keep this between you and me.

DONNIEMAC
But…

Sir.

TWENTY TWO – THE MESS

The Russian dolls look on.

Every man is focused on a much drawn and redrawn diagram.

Every man has a pen/pencil or finger to resketch…

NEWDADMIKE
look…if the torpedo didn't fire…

CASANOVAKEN
Fucking Soviets !!!
They pay shit money…

> *DONNIE MAC joins them with another secret.*

> *…he starts making tea.*

You got to figure those lads have thought…

'fuck it…shit money…cut corners…shit torpedo-firing
mechanism…fuck it!'

CASANOVA
Bastards

NEWDADMIKE
So it just blew *inside* in *this*
compartment here…
it blows *back…*
takes out *all* the control room…
so she's out of control…

OTHERS
Yeah…we've *got* that…

NEWDADMIKE
Keep *with* me…
Okay…it detonates *all* their bloody torpedoes…
But
But
Does it get their nuclear reactors…?
………?

> *ALL struck to silence by this.*

DONNIE BLACK
No.

No…or right now *we'd* be…

ALL
In need of a *lot* of sunscreen
Right!

NEWDADMIKE
So
If the nuclear reactors are safe…
Anybody in these three aft compartments…
Might still be

DONNIE MAC
Alive

> *All sit and take this in…*
>
> *Then.*
>
> *As one…*
>
> *Back poring over the diagram…*

NEWDADMIKE
Look at that!
That's got to be an escape hatch…
That's *got* to be an escape hatch!!!!

DONNIE BLACK
She's only in 115 meters for fuck sake!

If somebody goes down…locks on…
They could get them out…

DONNIE MAC
Not *us*
We're an *attack* vessel

CASANOVAKEN
We could do it with one of our LR5's like that! (*Fingersnap.*)

> *Everybody agrees…*

ALL
LR5   Ideal!

DONNIE MAC
Probably have to be a fucking *Russian* rescue
But their fucking *Priz* rescue subs are too fucking shit to save
their own fucking shit boats

Everybody agrees.

CASANOVA
Bastards

Yanks could surely take a look

DONNIE MAC
Dream on

NEWDADMIKE
Can't *we* do anything?

Nip back…sniff around?

Where's The Boss at?

CASANOVA
He's thinking

But what the fuck can he do?

THE BOSS
(*Pipe…*)

Do you hear there, Captain speaking.
Gentlemen, we have received no instructions from command
Regarding assisting *Kursk*.
we are therefore with regret
unable to rescue any putative survivors on *Kursk*.
Collected Data indicates that it is doubtful there are now any
survivors.
I'm sorry, lads
I know you will be very frustrated.

Let us all think of the men of the Kursk and their families
During Four o'clockers

Let's have the last of the scones, Coxn.

DONNIE BLACK/COXN
Sir

> *Goes for the scones.*

> *Everybody looks at DONNIE MAC, who knew what THE BOSS was going to decide...*

DONNE MAC
(*Loses it...*)

What the fuck can he do?

???

Disobey orders?

???

Scones!

Brilliant!

Let's all eat our bloody scones!!!!

DONNIE BLACK
MacNaugton.

DONNIE MAC
Yes, Coxn.

DONNIE BLACK
Sort your shit out.
Now.
Or you'll be down my office.
Right?

DONNIE MAC
Yes sir.

> *And they all sit down with tea and scones.*

> *They are all silent.*

> *Their heads and hearts on Kursk...*

> *Until...*

NEWDADMIKE gets up suddenly…

Exit towards bunks.

DONNIEMAC
Bloody secrecy!
Bloody secret bloody stuff!

DONNIE BLACK
Fucking Atlantis.
Fucking trying to live in fucking *Atlantis*

DONNIE MAC
This is mad!
This is bloody mad!
Pass me a bloody scone!

He lifts his tea cup towards the Russian dolls.

Fucking sorry, boys

TWENTY-THREE – IN WHICH WE DREAM…

Radio and SONAR and boat running continues as…

Around the boat…

Everyone else at stations…

*DONNIE BLACK reading…*Musee des Beaux Arts –
W H Auden…

NEWDADMIKE sleeping…

DONNIE BLACK
'About suffering they were never wrong,
The Old Masters; how well, they understood
Its human position; how it takes place
While someone else is eating or opening a window or just walking dully along;
How, when the aged are reverently, passionately waiting
For the miraculous birth, there always must be
Children who did not specially want it to happen, skating
On a pond at the edge of the wood:

They never forgot
That even the dreadful martyrdom must run its course
Anyhow in a corner, some untidy spot
Where the dogs go on with their doggy life and the torturer's
horse
Scratches its innocent behind on a tree.
In Breughel's Icarus, for instance: how everything turns away
Quite leisurely from the disaster; the ploughman may
Have heard the splash, the forsaken cry,
But for him it was not an important failure; the sun shone
As it had to on the white legs disappearing into the green
Water; and the expensive delicate ship that must have seen
Something amazing, a boy falling out of the sky,
had somewhere to get to and sailed calmly on.'

Meanwhile…

NEWDADMIKE
(*His bunk becomes an iron coffin…*) When did I die?
When did I die?
When did I die?
No I'm not dead I'm not dead but but but…
Oh *fuck*! I'm in a coffin/somebody's put me in a coffin…
Not wood it's not wood it's iron oh fuck it's iron!!!

DONNIEBLACK
Mike!

You're shouting…

NEWDADMIKE responds in his sleep.

He's quiet for a bit…

Then…

NEWDADMIKE
What's all this *earth??????*
I can't…*breathe…*

He struggles for air…

A strong green creeper starts growing round him and his bunk…

what the…a *creeper!!!*
what the…
hell?????

> *It grows all over him, like chains holding him down…*

What?

> *The creeper sprouts an intense, perfect white flower.*

> *This is perfect white flower.*

This *perfect* white flower!!!

> *He looks behind him. A small girl is coming towards him with a bucket and spade.*

This is for *you*

Who are you?

Where did you come from then?

Are you going to do some digging in the sand?

Is it *you* Madison????

All grown up……???

DONNIE BLACK
Mike, mate…you're making a lot of noise…

NEWDADMIKE
What can you see (*End of bunk.*) there?

> *DONNIE BLACK looks.*

> *Looks back at NEWDADMIKE…*

Is there somebody standing   *there*?

> *DONNIE BLACK/COXN looks.*

DONNIE BLACK/COXN
You're over tired.
Whatever you're seeing lad, it's just a bad dream.
Go back to sleep.
It's alright.

And NEWDADMIKE does.

As DONNIE BLACK knows it's not alright.

TWENTY-FOUR – THE OUTBREATH...

DONNIE MAC is in THE BOSS's cabin.

RADIO OPS/DONNIE MAC...
Lot of conversation back and forth... Sir
Nobody's mentioning *Kursk* by name...
They're pretending something very minor's
Put a dint in their perfection...
Sonar says
Something's been down...
Small submersible...no identification...
Sniffing around her for a few hours.../

THE BOSS
Roger that.

DONNIE MAC/RADIO OPS
Left and surfaced
About an hour ago...

THE BOSS
Roger that.

DONNIE MAC/RADIO OPS
Sir.

THE BOSS
Here we are
Here we go.

> *He gives the order to leave the area.*
>
> *DONNIE MAC stands by while he does it.*
>
> *In darkness, we are in the ninth compartment on Kursk.*

VASILY
Dmitri...you okay?

DMITRI
I'm writing our names

VASILY
What are our chances?

DMITRI
Not very good now, Vasily.

And the sounds of our boat retreating from…

The sound of breathing.

It becomes

Shallower

harder.

It stops.

TWENTY-FIVE – THE END-OF-MISSION PARTY

Somebody's mixed tape …

THE REAL SLIM SHADY by EMINEM…

as…

Begins with a mock trial…

All very smartly dressed…

All very grave…

Russian dolls are at the party, also a bit dressed up.

Great trouble has been taken.

DONNIE MAC
With three days to go before you are
Re-released among human beings…
Do you understand the charges?

CASANOVAKEN
Yes your honour

DONNIE MAC
You've been tried
By a jury of your peers..

DONNIE BLACK
(*To Russian Dolls*.) Thank you Ivan Ivan Ivan Ivan Ivan Ivan
and Igor for your *unstinting* vigilance…

The dolls look back with unstinting vigilance.

DONNIE MAC
Tried…
and found guilty
Of
Masturbation in the first degree

CASANOVAKEN
Yes your honour

DONNIE MAC
Masturbation in the first degree
with *a wristwatch*

CASANOVAKEN
I'm particularly remorseful about the wristwatch
Your honour

DONNIE BLACK
Wouldn't have apprehended the culprit
But for the wristwatch, your honour

DONNIE MAC
You abused this innocent toilet

CASANOVAKEN
Yes

DONNIE BLACK
You *animal!*

DONNIE MAC
You understand…
You will have to make an honest woman of her…

CASANOVAKEN
Yes, your honour

DONNIE MAC
Do you Ken Casanova Eustace Webster
Take this urinal
To be your loyal wedded wife
To have and to hold
For ever and ever amen?

CASANOVAKEN
I do

Until we dock, anyway…

DONNIE BLACK
You may kiss the bride

CASANOVAKEN
I'll marry it, but I'll be fucked if 'll kiss it!

> *They upend him and make him kiss his lawful-wedded wife.*
>
> *Party poppers, drinks, party time!*
>
> *As our boys fool about…eat special stuff etc…*

THE BOSS
(*Pipe…*)

OM Warboys. Captain's Cabin

NEWDADMIKE
What the fuck…?

> *He goes to THE BOSS's cabin.*
>
> *DONNIE MAC watches.*

CASANOVAKEN
What?

DONNIE MAC
Nothing

You might need to stand by…

> *In THE BOSS's cabin.*

THE BOSS
Mike. Sit down.

NEWDADMIKE sits down.

CASANOVAKEN
What?

THE BOSS
I'm afraid there's been some bad news.

Hands MIKE the gram…

MIKE reads the message from NAVAL COMMAND…

MESSAGE
To OM Michael Warboys.
We regret to inform him that his daughter
Madison Emily Hannah Warboys
Died unexpectedly in her cot at approximately 3.00am
On the night of 7th September 2000.
We offer our most sincere condolences.

CASANOVAKEN
Fuck no…

DONNIE BLACK
Gentlemen
A toast to another good mission

ALL
Another good mission

DONNIE BLACK
A safe return

ALL
A safe return

DONNIE BLACK
A toast to our Russian friends…
Good missions and safe returns for them too.
Peaceful sleep for those who don't return.
Brilliant compensation for their families.

Silence.

DONNIE MAC
Spa-koy-nee no chi

ALL
Spa-koy-nee-no chi

Everybody is silent. DONNIE BLACK tries a poetic poultice…

DONNIE BLACK
(*Quotes.*) 'In the intervals
Of rough wind and rain
The first cherry blossoms'

DONNIE MAC
What the fuck is *that?*

DONNIE BLACK
Something fucking *meaningful*
Fucking *haiku*, mate…
Something *big* and *meaningful* condensed into a small space.
Fucking *poetry.*

TWENTY-SIX – A HELICOPTER ARRIVES

We hear the entire CREW LIST of the KURSK K-141 as…

THE BOSS reads…with appropriate attitude to…

CITATION
Statement by the Kremlin in August 2000
…or courage and heroism shown during performance of a
sailor's duty, the Kursk commanding officer Captain G.P.
Lyachin has been given the rank of Hero of the Russian
federation [posthumously] on 26th August 2000.
All 118 crew members are awarded the Courage order
[posthumously] and are inscribed for ever in the memory of
the 7th Division of the Ist Submarine Flotilla of the Northern
Fleet…

First compartment
1. Senior Midshipman Abdulkhadur Ildarov [Dagestan
    Republic]

2. Midshipman Alexei Zubov [Ukraine]
3. Seaman Ivan Nefedkov [Sverdlovsk Region]
4. Seaman Maxim Borzhov [Vladimir Region]
5. Seaman Alexei Shulgin [Archangel Region]
6. Senior Lieutenant Arnold Borisov [Dagestan Republic]
7. Mamed Gadjiiev [Dagestan Republic

Second Compartment
Visiting from the 7th Submarine Division Headquarters:
1. Captain First rank Vladimir Bagriantsev [Crimea
2. Captain Second Rank Yury Shepetnov [Crimea]
3. Captain Second Rank Viktor Belogun [Ukraine]
4. Captain Second Rank Vasily Isaenko [Crimea]
5. Captain Third Rank Marat Baygari [St.Petersburg]

Crew:
6. Captain First Rank Gennady Lyachin [Volgograd region]
7. Captain Second Rank Sergei Dudko [Belorussia]
8. Captain Second Rank Alexander Shubin [Crimea]
9. Captain-Lietenant Maxim Safonov [Moscow]
10. Senior Lietenant Sergei Tylik [Murmansk]
11. Senior Lietenant Vadim Bubniv [Ulyanovsk Region]
12. Captain Third Rank Andrei Silogava [Crimea]
13. Senior Lietenant Alexei Shevchuk [Murmansk]
14. Senior Lietenant Andrei Onarin [St.Petersburg]
15. Senior Boris Geletin [Murmansk]
16. Senior Lieutenant Sergei Uzky [Archangle Region]
17. Captain Second Rank Yury Sablin [Crimea]

As…

CASANOVAKEN meanwhile packs his things for him,

Meets him at the foot of a ladder…

Accompanies him up …

Sound of HELICOPTER arriving far away…

HELICOPTER
Submarine submarine this is Whisky Bravo

OOW/DONNIE MAC
(*On radio.*) Whisky bravo this is submarine submarine over

HELICOPTER
Submarine submarine this Whisky Bravo ETA ten minutes

OOW/DONNIE MAC
submarine submarine roger ETA 10 minutes

(*On broadcast…*) Do you hear there helicopter transfer party, muster fwd on one deck.

> *NEWDADMIKE for transfer and CASANOVA with an earthing strop and a bag carrier in the control room and DONNIE BLACK takes details. On a board with 'NAME TIME UP AND TIME DOWN.*

COXN/DONNIEBLACK
bridge ship control

OOW/DONNIE MAC
BRIDGE

COXN/DONNIE BLACK
Transfer party mustered in the control room

OOW/DONNIE MAC
roger ready send up the transfer party

COXN/DONNIE BLACK
OK up you go straight to the bridge.

HELICOPTER
submarine submarine this is Whisky Bravo have you in sight

> *HELICOPTER sounds grows very loud as.*

ETA 1 minute.

COXN/DONNIE BLACK
Whisky Bravo roger ETA one minute

> *Dials captain's cabin and tells him helicopter rendezvous takes place in a minute's time.*

OOW/DONNIE MAC
Ship control, officer of the watch

COXN/DONNIE BLACK
SHIP Control

OOW/DONNIE MAC
transfer complete, coming below. (*They get to the bottom of the tower.*)

NEWDADMIKE disappears upwards into non-subspace.

DONNIE BLACK and CASANOVA watch him...

A man's hand takes the paper submarine off the mobile.

Lights fade

The list of the dead Kursk submariners continues.

Silence.

END OF PLAY.